KNOWLEDGE ENCYCLOPEDIA
CHEMISTRY & ELEMENTS

© Wonder House Books 2024

All rights reserved. No part of this book may be reproduced or transmitted in any form by any means, electronic or mechanical, including photocopying and recording, or by any information storage and retrieval system except as may be expressly permitted in writing by the publisher.

(An imprint of Prakash Books)

contact@wonderhousebooks.com

Disclaimer: The information contained in this encyclopedia has been collated with inputs from subject experts. All information contained herein is true to the best of the Publisher's knowledge.

ISBN : 9789354401602

Table of Contents

The Basis of All Things	3
What Makes Up Matter	4–5
The Periodic Table	6–7
States of Matter	8–9
Purification Methods	10–11
Chemical Reactions and Bonds	12–13
Acids, Bases, and pH	14–15
Catalysts	16
Metals	17
Hydrogen and Helium	18
Noble Gases	19
Nitrogen	20
Oxygen	21
Carbon	22–23
Sulphur and Phosphorus	24
Silicon, Semiconductors, and Ceramics	25
Currency Metals	26
Iron and Steel	27
Polymers, Plastics, and Rubber	28–29
Nuclear Chemistry	30
Green Chemistry	31
Word Check	32

THE BASIS OF ALL THINGS

When you hear the word 'chemical', do you think of coloured liquid sloshing around in a glass flask in a laboratory or of large tankers with 'Hazardous' written on the side?

Yet, did you realise that you too are made of chemicals—proteins, carbohydrates, lipids, nucleic acids, and water? Or that all our food is chemical? Indeed, all matter in the Universe is made of chemicals, as long as it is made of atoms, molecules, or ions. Apart from some stars that are made of subatomic particles, everything in our Universe is made of different combinations of about 100 elements that came into being the day the Universe itself did, with the Big Bang.

Once upon a time, alchemy was popular all over the world, as humans tried to find out the secrets of the material world and turn everyday things into gold. They finally found that it was impossible to do so, but in the process, they discovered various other useful things—how to purify materials, the nature of chemical reactions, the uses of petroleum, and even the chemical basis of life. And that became the modern science of chemistry.

▼ Modern chemistry owes its origins to ancient alchemists' quest for gold

What Makes Up Matter

In the past, people thought that the Universe was made of five elements: earth, water, fire, air, and ether. Today, we know that none of these are elements. Air is a mixture of gases, and earth is a complicated mixture of solids, liquids, and gases. Water and ether are compounds, while fire is simply the light emitted when a compound is **oxidised** at high temperature. Let's read on to find out what these words mean.

Element

An element is anything that cannot be broken down into simpler things by ordinary **chemical reactions**. So far, we know of 118 elements, of which about 20 are artificial elements made in nuclear laboratories. The rest all occur naturally. The most common elements on our planet are nitrogen—which encompasses most of our atmosphere, oxygen, silicon, aluminium, and iron in the Earth's crust. The core of our planet is made of a molten mix of iron and nickel, and deep inside is a ball of solid iron.

Chemists use one or two letters which represent elements when writing down chemical reactions. These letters are known as chemical symbols that are based on the elements' names.

For most elements, the first letter of their English name, such as C (carbon) or O (oxygen) is their symbol. Some elements have two letters, like Cl for chlorine. Elements known to science before the year 1800 have different names in different languages. Therefore, scientists use symbols based on their Latin names, such as K for potassium which is *kalium* in Latin, or Na for sodium which is *natrium* in Latin. Most metals and elements discovered recently have names ending in -ium—such as sodium or rutherfordium, while non-metals have names ending in -on, -gen, etc.—such as argon or nitrogen.

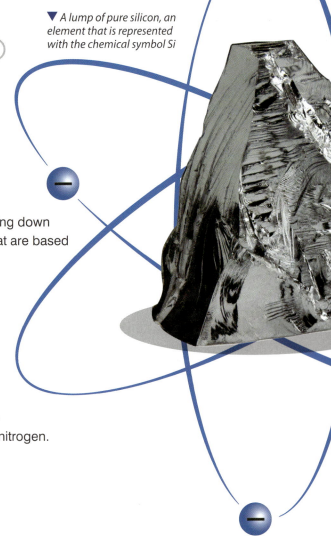

▼ *A lump of pure silicon, an element that is represented with the chemical symbol Si*

▼ *There are just 118 elements, but millions of different chemical compounds*

Compound

A compound is a substance made of two or more elements that can be broken down into its constituent elements by ordinary chemical reactions. Some compounds, such as deoxyribonucleic acid (DNA), can be very complicated and made of billions of atoms of different elements. A compound is written using the symbols of the elements in it, and numbers which depict the ratio these elements are found in. (The numbers are written in subscript after the symbol of each element in a compound).

For example, common salt is made of sodium (Na) and chloride (Cl) in equal proportions, so it is written as NaCl. Water is made of two parts hydrogen (H) and one part oxygen (O), so it is written as H_2O.

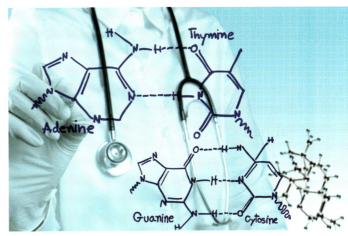

▲ DNA is a complicated chemical compound made of carbon (C), hydrogen (H), oxygen (O), nitrogen (N), and phosphorus (P)

Atom

Every element has a number of traits by which it can be distinguished. These are called its chemical properties, which include things such as mass, reactivity, density, and hardness. All of these in turn depend on the atoms that make it up. An atom is the smallest thing in the Universe that exists by itself at ordinary temperatures. In turn, an atom is made of three things called subatomic particles:

1. Electrons, which weigh almost zero, have a tiny negative electric charge and revolve around the **nucleus** (like the Earth revolves around the Sun).
2. Protons, which have a tiny positive electric charge.
3. Neutrons, with no charge. Protons and neutrons live in the centre of the atom, forming its nucleus.

An atom of an element always has the same number of protons and electrons, while atoms of different elements have different numbers of protons (and electrons). So helium has two protons and two electrons, while helium and lithium have two and three protons and electrons respectively.

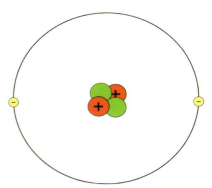

▲ Model of a helium atom, which has two protons, neutrons, and electrons

Molecule

A molecule is made of two or more atoms that have come together in a chemical reaction. A molecule may be made of atoms of the same element or different elements. Some elements—such as nitrogen, oxygen, or chlorine—can exist in nature only as molecules.

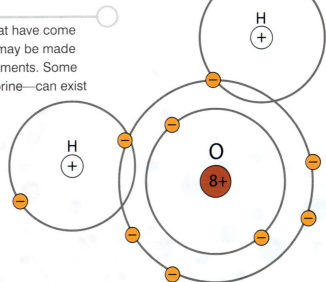

▶ A water molecule is made of hydrogen and oxygen atoms that have come together in a chemical reaction

The Periodic Table

All atoms are made of electrons, protons, and neutrons. The number of protons in an atom—called its atomic number—decide which element it belongs to. For example, if there is only one proton in an atom, then it is an atom of hydrogen; if it has six protons, then it is an atom of carbon, and so on. The number of protons and neutrons together make up an element's atomic mass. Atoms of the same element may have one or more additional neutrons, which increase its atomic mass, but not its atomic number. Such atoms are called isotopes of the element.

Elements can be lined up based on their increasing atomic number. Scientists originally discovered that the chemical properties of elements were similar in periods of eight, so lithium, sodium, and potassium are similar to each other as highly reactive metals, while helium, neon, and argon are similar to each other as unreactive gases. This is now known as the periodic law, and the table is called the periodic table.

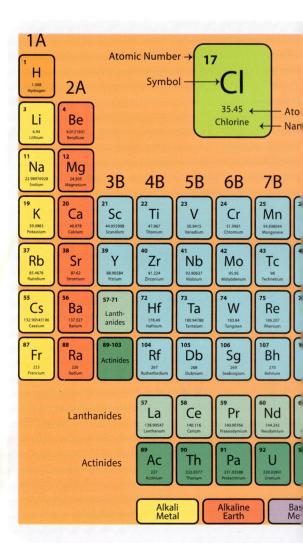

Hydrogen
Hydrogen (H) is the simplest element made of one proton and electron and no neutron. This element is abundantly available in the Universe and is known as the mother of all elements.

Alkali Metals
These are some of the most reactive elements in nature. They do not exist in their pure state, but are always found as compounds known as salts.

Alkaline Earth Metals
After alkali metals, these are the most reactive elements. Magnesium (Mg) is needed for photosynthesis, and calcium (Ca) is needed for our bone formation.

Transition Metals
These make up the biggest section of the periodic table. They have chemical properties between alkali metals and non-metals, so they behave like metals sometimes and like non-metals other times. They form some of the most industrially useful chemicals, such as copper, iron, and manganese.

🏅 Incredible Individuals

The Russian scientist Dmitri Mendeleev (1834–1907) created the periodic table in 1869, after studying the properties of all the elements known in his time. He even predicted the chemical properties of elements that were unknown at the time, such as gallium. When gallium was discovered in 1875, it had the same properties Mendeleev had predicted for it!

▲ *In 1969, Russia printed a stamp honouring Dmitri Mendeleev*

CHEMISTRY & ELEMENTS

Post-transition Metals
These are metals that are closer to semiconductors and are relatively inert. Aluminium (Al) and lead (Pb) have many uses while the rest are used as semiconductor dopes. Transition metals are on their left in the periodic table, while metalloids are represented on their right.

Metalloids
These are also known as semiconductors. They are used in modern electronics.

Non-metals
This is a diverse bunch of elements. Apart from selenium (Se), they are the elements most needed for life, such as carbon (C), nitrogen (N), oxygen (O), sulphur (S), and phosphorus (P). They are usually plastic (i.e. they will not regain their shape if bent) and cannot conduct electricity, as opposed to metals and metalloids that are elastic and can conduct electricity.

Halogens
These are the most reactive non-metallic elements. We use them for many purposes such as making lamp fillings, cleaning agents, and plastics; and they often partner with alkali metals in forming salts.

Noble Gases
These elements exist as gas in the natural state. Since they do not react with anything, they are called inert gases; and as they are not very abundant, they are also called rare gases.

Lanthanides
These elements are also called rare earths. They have many uses in modern electronic devices such as semiconductors and switches.

Actinides
Most of these are radioactive elements. Uranium (U) is the most important and is used in nuclear reactors to make electricity, while others like plutonium (Pu) are used in nuclear weapons.

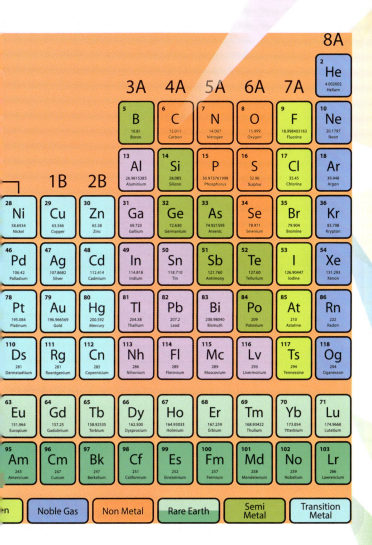

▲ The periodic table showing all the 118 elements

▼ Atomic structure for Hydrogen, Oxygen, Carbon, and Nitrogen

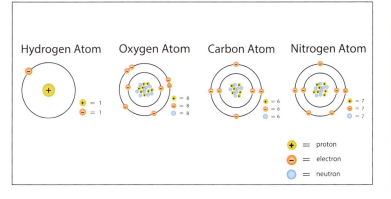

In Real Life

An element that is yet to be discovered is named after its atomic number using Latin numbers and '-ium'. So, element no. 119 is called un-un-enn-ium. Once an element's discovery is verified by other scientists, the people who first discovered it are free to give it any name they like.

States of Matter

Chemists define matter as anything that can be touched or felt. At any given temperature and pressure, matter will exist in a phase (also called a state of matter), in which its atoms or molecules have a certain amount of freedom to move and can be separated from another phase by physical means. The natural phase of all materials is their physical condition at 20°C–25°C ('room temperature'), and atmospheric pressure at sea level. For example, water is liquid in its natural state, but it turns to gas (steam) when heated above 100°C, and solid (ice) when cooled below 0°C.

If you heat or cool a material, at some temperature, it will change from one phase to another. Scientists call this a phase transition. Every material will change into another phase at a specific transition temperature. In daily life, there are two main transition temperatures. The melting point is when a solid becomes liquid, and when the opposite happens (liquid becomes solid), it is called the freezing point. Further, the boiling point is when a liquid becomes gas, and the condensation point is when gas becomes liquid.

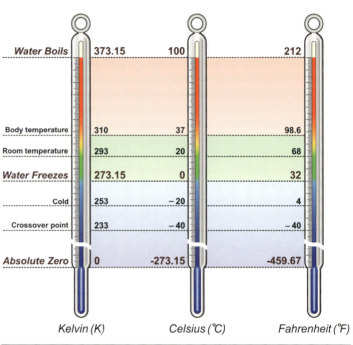

▲ Did you know that the Celsius scale is based on the melting and boiling points of water?

▶ Steam is the gas form of water. It is used to power engines and turbines

Gas

This is a state of matter when all the atoms or molecules of a pure substance have complete freedom to move; imagine a classroom when the teacher is absent. This is called **fluidity**. Nitrogen (N), oxygen (O), hydrogen (H), the **halogens** (F, Cl, Br, I, At, Ts), and the **noble** gases (He, Ar, Xe, Kr, Rn, Og) are elemental gases, while carbon dioxide (CO_2), ammonia (NH_3), sulphur dioxide (SO_2), and methane (CH_4) are compound gases.

CHEMISTRY & ELEMENTS

Plasma

A plasma is a special kind of gas that exists when there is very high electric current. Many kinds of atoms, especially those of metals, lose an electron or two and become positively charged (since now they have more protons). Other kinds of atoms gain an extra electron and become negatively charged. Both kinds of charged atoms are called ions. Plasmas are used in Plasma TVs and many other electrical applications.

◀ Water dissolves so many things that it is called the universal solvent

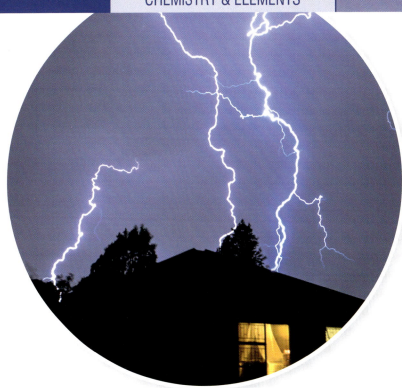

▲ Lightning lights up the sky around 50–100 times per second around the planet

Liquid

This is a state of matter when the atoms or molecules have lost some freedom to move; similar to a parade of soldiers moving under the officer's orders. Liquids move at a speed known as their **viscosity**—the more of it they have, the less fluid they are. Mercury (Hg) and iodine (I) are the only elemental liquids at room temperature. On the other hand, thousands of compounds are liquids at room temperature. Water (H_2O) is the best-known liquid. Many liquids are used as **solvents**, in which other solids or liquids (such as sugar or salt) can be dissolved for carrying out chemical reactions. You may often hear or read that glass is a very viscous liquid, but that is not true. Glass is an amorphous solid, that is, it has no internal structure.

Solid

When there's no freedom to move at all—like standing to attention for the national anthem—the atoms or molecules become a solid. Solids come in two forms: crystal, in which the atoms are arranged in rows and columns (called lattices) like soldiers in a parade; or amorphous, in which there is no organisation. One glass-like substance commonly called crystal is quartz, a mineral whose molecules are arranged in a regular lattice, which is transparent. Most elements and solid compounds are crystalline, such as sugar, salt, metals, and rocks. Many others, often made from living things, are amorphous, such as wood, chalk, cloth, and paper. Earth is a mixture of both kinds.

▲ Ice is the crystalline form of solid water, while snow is its amorphous form

Absolute Zero

The coldest temperature possible is –273.15°C, at which all the atoms and molecules of a substance completely freeze over. This is called absolute zero. In 1995, scientists found that near this temperature, atoms are no longer separate but merge to form a Bose-Einstein Condensate. Satyendra Nath Bose and Albert Einstein had predicted this in 1924. The Kelvin Scale of Temperature used by scientists is based on Absolute Zero. On this scale, –273.15°C is the same as 0°K (Kelvin), while 0°C is written as 273.15°K.

Purification Methods

When all the atoms or molecules in a material are of the same kind, it is called pure. In real life, nothing is ever 100% pure. There are always other things called impurities that are mixed in. When there are lots of impurities, it is impossible to predict what will happen when the material is used for chemical reactions, or for making things. Therefore, chemists use purification methods to make a material as pure as humanly possible. Here are a few important ones, though there are many more.

🔍 Sedimentation

This process uses gravity to separate solids from liquids. If you leave muddy water undisturbed in a glass, the mud will settle down and leave a clear layer of water above.

A machine called a **centrifuge** helps sedimentation happen faster by spinning mixtures in special tubes at very high speeds. The solid collected at the bottom is called sediment. Centrifugation is used in laboratories and chemical plants after a chemical reaction has produced a substance that is not soluble in water.

◀ Centrifugation is used to separate plasma from blood cells before the plasma can be given to a patient who needs it

🔍 Filtration

This is a method that makes use of the sizes of materials. A filter is a material that has holes of a certain size. Anything smaller than those holes will pass through, while bigger things will not. Filtration is used to separate floating particles from liquids and gases. When two solids are separated, it is called sieving.

Adsorption is a method by which impurities stick to a filter (usually finely powdered carbon) while water passes through.

▶ Air conditioners have filters fitted in them to remove dust and other particles by adsorption

▲ Water is purified in a treatment plant using several methods before it gets to your house

CHEMISTRY & ELEMENTS

Distillation

This is a method that makes use of the boiling point of a liquid. An impure liquid, like tap water, is boiled in a special distillation still. The water boils off, leaving solid impurities behind. At the other end of the still, the steam is condensed back to water.

One of the best-known methods for distillation is fractional distillation. Using this process, a mixture of two liquids, whose boiling points are far apart, is separated. For example, ethanol (C_2H_6O) boils at 78°C, while water boils at 100°C. By heating a mixture of ethanol and water at just above 78°C, ethanol can be distilled from water.

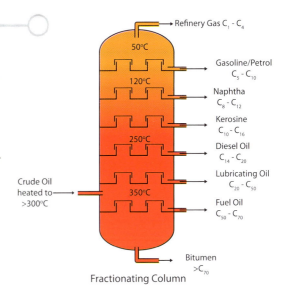

▲ *Fractional distillation is used to separate crude oil (petroleum) into useful chemicals. This is also called refining*

★ Incredible Individuals

Cleopatra the Alchemist (not to be confused with the queen of the same name) is believed to have lived in Egypt around the 2nd or 3rd century ce. She invented the alembic, a glass vessel used for distillation even today.

Crystallisation

Try this: add salt to water in increasing amounts and watch it dissolve. After some time, the salt will stop dissolving with water. This is called saturation. If you heat this solution, the undissolved salt will dissolve, and you can keep adding more salt as the water heats further. Stop adding salt when you reach the boiling point. Now let the solution cool. It has now reached **supersaturation**. If you add a grain of salt to the solution now, you will see highly structured crystals of salt forming in the solution. This is called crystallisation and is used to purify soluble solids from supersaturated solutions.

▲ *Sea salt is made by evaporating seawater, and then purified by re-dissolving it in fresh water and crystallising it*

💡 Isn't It Amazing!

Crystallisation is used to study the molecular structure of chemical compounds by throwing X-rays on a purified crystal. The pattern made by the X-ray is then analysed through mathematics. In this way, Rosalind Franklin found the structure of DNA.

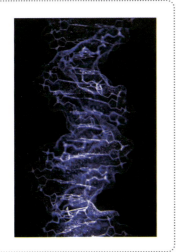

▶ *The structure of DNA was found by shining X-rays on it*

Sublimation

Some solids directly turn to gas when heated without going through the liquid phase. This is called sublimation. Sublimation can be used to separate two solids, if one of them becomes gas on being heated. Sublimation in vacuum is used to purify the materials used in electronics.

Chemical Reactions and Bonds

Chemical reactions occur when one chemical meets another under specific conditions. The chemicals going into a reaction are called reactants, while those that are formed after the reaction are called products. To understand them, let's learn how electrons are arranged in an atom. They revolve around the nucleus, but different electrons move in different **orbitals**, just like the planets move around the Sun in different orbits. The farther an electron is from the nucleus, the less it is attracted to it. Reaction speeds then vary and depend on temperature.

Each orbital must have its electrons in pairs. If it doesn't, it is said to be unstable. Apart from noble gases, all elements have at least one unstable orbital, that is, they have only one electron. This unstable orbital is what causes chemical reactions.

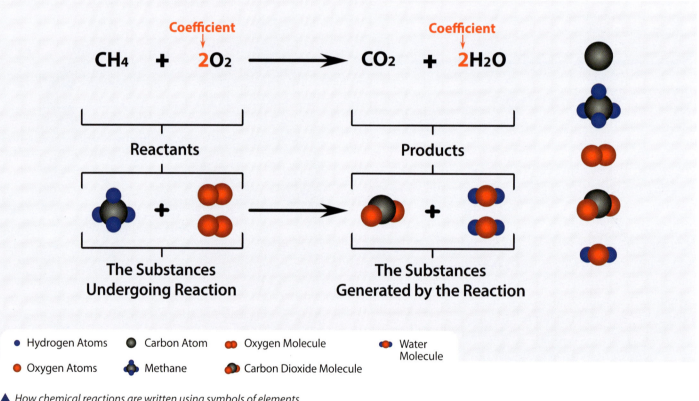

▲ How chemical reactions are written using symbols of elements

🔍 Ionising Reactions

Unstable orbitals make an atom 'behave' in either of two ways. If the electron is far from the nucleus, the atom it belongs to may simply give it away to an atom that wants it. It now becomes an ion. As it has more protons than electrons, it has a positive electrical charge, so it is called a cation. Hydrogen and most metals form cations.

In the case where an atom takes electrons from other atoms, the receiving atom becomes an ion with a negative electrical charge called an anion. Most non-metals, halogens, and metalloids become anions.

A chemical reaction in which cations and anions are formed is called a redox reaction or an ionising reaction. The element or compound that gains electrons is said to have become reduced, while the element or compound that gave up electrons becomes oxidised. The resulting product is called a **salt**. The salt added to your food is just one kind of salt, sodium chloride ($NaCl$).

CHEMISTRY & ELEMENTS

Ionic Bond

An ionising reaction creates one cation and one anion. They attract each other strongly because of opposite charges, forming an ionic compound. This attraction is strong enough to keep them bonded to each other, so it is called an electrovalent bond or an ionic bond. In the solid state, an ionic compound forms regular crystals.

Non-Ionic Reactions

The unstable orbitals of non-metallic elements can behave in another way. Instead of losing or gaining electrons, atoms of non-metals often 'share' electrons. This way, each atom's unstable orbital gets to have two electrons. A chemical reaction in which this happens is called a non-ionic reaction. The most common example of this is burning, when oxygen in the air reacts with heated fuels such as gasoline or diesel. The scientific name for this is combustion and it is used in the combustion engines that power cars.

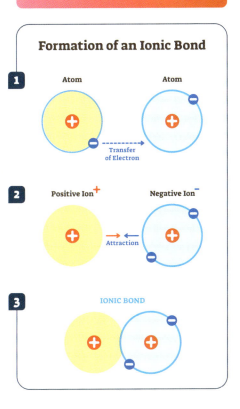

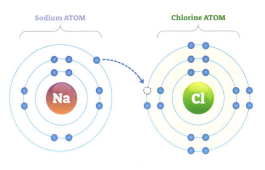

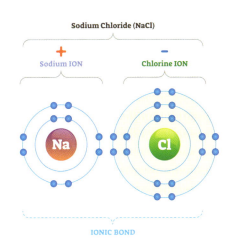

▲ A redox reaction leads to the formation of a compound with an electrovalent bond between its ions

Covalent Bond

A non-ionic reaction creates no ions but the atoms still stick around each other and share their electrons. The bond between them is called a covalent bond. Covalent compounds are often gases or liquids. In the solid state, they are often amorphous.

Hydrogen Bond

In water, hydrogen atoms share electrons with oxygen. The larger oxygen nucleus pulls the shared electrons closer to it, gaining a tiny negative charge. Hydrogen gains a matching positive charge. This makes hydrogen atoms weakly attract oxygen atoms from another water molecule. This is called a hydrogen bond, which is weaker than covalent bonds or ionic bonds.

Incredible Individuals

John Dalton (1766–1844) believed that the chemical properties of elements are because of the structure of their atoms. Until his time, it was believed that all elements were made of the same kinds of atoms, but he showed that each element has its own different atomic structure. Today, we know this as atomic theory.

▶ John Dalton laid the foundation of modern chemistry

Acids, Bases, and pH

In most books and films, an acid is shown as a coloured liquid fuming in a laboratory, or something that causes an upset stomach. However, scientists define acids and bases in a very different way. Acids and bases form much of the groundwork of modern chemistry and have hundreds of uses. They are often used to convert raw materials into the plastics, paints, medicines, preservatives, dyes, and many other chemicals we use in daily life. The balance of acids and bases in our body is an important part of staying healthy.

Acid

Scientists define an acid as something that easily gives up a hydrogen ion (H^+) or ends up with extra electrons at the end of a reaction. Another definition of an acid is that it is any chemical in which one or more hydrogen atoms can be replaced by a positively charged ion (cation). The three most common acids used for chemical reactions are hydrochloric acid (HCl, which is also found in your stomach), sulphuric acid (H_2SO_4), and nitric acid (HNO_3).

Fatty acids, which are made of carbon molecules, do not dissolve in water. All others dissolve in water and break up into anions and hydrogen ions:

$$HCl + H_2O \rightarrow H^+ + Cl^- + H_2O$$

▼ Many compound gases dissolve in water vapour to form acid droplets

Base

A base is the opposite of an acid. It is something that easily takes up a hydrogen ion (H^+) or ends up with fewer electrons at the end of a reaction. The three most common bases used for chemical reactions are sodium hydroxide (NaOH, also called caustic soda), potassium hydroxide (KOH, also called caustic potash), and ammonium hydroxide (NH_4OH). Bases that react really fast are called alkalis.

Bases dissolve in water and break up into cations and hydroxide ions:

$$NaOH + H_2O \rightarrow Na^+ + OH^- + H_2O$$

◀ Throughout the world, there are lakes that have become alkaline, like the Little Alkali Lake situated in California, USA

CHEMISTRY & ELEMENTS

💡 Isn't It Amazing!

Aqua regia is a mix of hydrochloric and nitric acid used to dissolve the metals gold and platinum. In 1940, when the Nazis invaded Denmark, they wanted to seize the Nobel Prize medals given to Jewish scientists Max von Laue and James Franck—but they could not find them. Another scientist, George Hevesy, had dissolved them in aqua regia. After the war, the gold was recovered and cast into new medals.

🔍 Salt

A salt is formed when an acid reacts with a base by the neutralisation reaction:

$$NaOH + HCl + H_2O \rightarrow Na^+ + Cl^- + 2H_2O$$

Many acids and bases react very strongly with each other, releasing a lot of heat. Such reactions are called exothermic reactions.

▶ Sea salt is mostly sodium chloride

🔍 pH

pH stands for potential of Hydrogen. It is a way of determining how acidic or basic a solution is, by measuring the number of hydrogen ions present in it. The pH scale is inverse logarithmic, that is, an increase of 1 on the scale means that there are 10 times fewer hydrogen ions. Closely related to it is the pOH scale, which measures the number of hydroxyl (OH-) ions. At a pH of 7, there are equal number of hydrogen ions and **hydroxyl ions**, so the solution is said to be neutral. Below 7, the solution is acidic and above 7, it is basic or alkaline.

H_2SO_4

HNO_3

Trees killed by acid rain

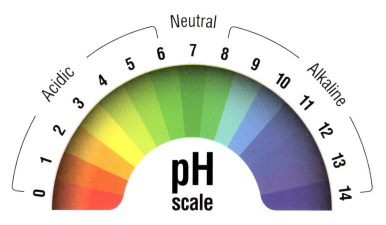

▲ The higher the pH, the fewer the hydrogen ions present

👤 In Real Life

Some chemicals change colours if the pH of their solution changes. They are therefore used as pH indicators. Your school lab may have pH papers, which are special paper strips soaked in chemical and dried. When dipped into an acidic or basic solution, the paper changes colour.

▲ A pH paper changing colour to show that there is alkali left over in a bar of soap, which may burn your skin

Catalysts

Some acids and bases react very easily and quickly with other things, so they are called strong acids and strong bases. Others react slowly, so they are called weak acids and weak bases. The ease with which a chemical reacts is called its **reactivity**. If you want to make a reaction go faster, you can heat the vessel containing the chemicals, or put a lot of pressure on it by placing a weight above it. Another way is by using a catalyst, a chemical that does not take part in the reaction or is re-formed at the end of the reaction. Among the most common catalysts in the world are enzymes—**proteins** created by our bodies while digesting food which help many other reactions inside our body.

Homogeneous catalysis happens when the catalyst and reactants are all in the same state of matter. For example, sodium bicarbonate ($NaHCO_3$) and citric acid ($C_6H_8O_7$) will not react with each other when they are in a dry form. When they are dissolved in water, the water acts as a catalyst and they react, forming carbon dioxide. This is used for making **antacids**.

$$NaHCO_3 + C_6H_8O_7 + H_2O \rightarrow NaC_6H_7O_7 + CO_2 + 2H_2O$$

Heterogeneous catalysis happens when the catalyst is in a different state of matter than the reactants. Graphite (a form of carbon), platinum (Pt), and palladium (Pd) are the most common catalysts. Iron (solid state) is used as a catalyst in the manufacture of ammonia from nitrogen and hydrogen (both gases).

▲ *Solid catalysts help increase the surface area and bring reactants together*

🔍 Enzymes

Enzymes work inside our bodies by a mechanism known as lock-and-key. There are thousands of enzymes in each of our cells and each enzyme catalyses only a single reaction. The enzyme's molecular structure has slots that allow different reactants to stick to it. Enzymes either join two reactants into one (called anabolism) or break a reactant into two (called catabolism). Anabolic enzymes are required for making proteins and other things that we need to grow, while catabolic enzymes are needed for digesting food and getting energy out of it. For example, pepsin, an enzyme made in our stomach, breaks down the proteins we eat.

▶ *Enzymes work by bringing reactants together and reducing activation energy*

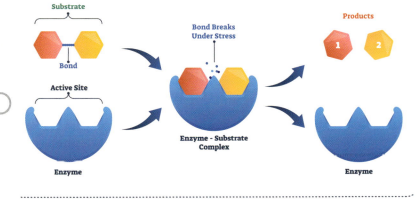

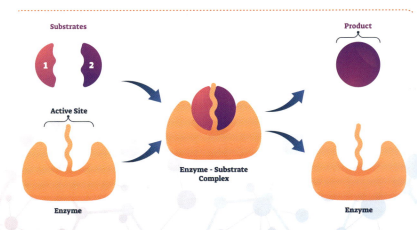

CHEMISTRY & ELEMENTS

Metals

Chemically, a metal is an element that can form a cation by giving up an electron, and a non-metal is an element that forms an anion by accepting an electron. A common property of metals is that they should malleable (easily hammered into sheets), or ductile (drawn into wires). They exist as crystalline solids in nature (except mercury, Hg), often do not react easily, and can readily conduct heat and electricity. They also have great tensile strength, that is, they can be stretched without breaking.

▲ Ingots or blocks of various metals

Silver, gold, copper, and iron are among the oldest metals known to humanity, along with bronze, an alloy of copper and tin. The history of humanity is divided into the Stone Age, the Bronze Age and the Iron Age. The Stone Age ended around 3300 BCE when humans discovered that they could make better tools out of metals instead of stone. As the hardest metallic substance available was bronze, the period is called the Bronze Age. Around 1200 BCE, humans discovered how to purify iron from its ore, thus starting the Iron Age. Iron is tougher and more flexible than bronze, and can be used for making many more things. We still live in the Iron Age.

Let's look at the periodic table on pages 6–7. Why do different kinds of metals take up so much space on it, and if they have common properties, why do they seem to be of different kinds?

🔍 Reactive Metals

Chemically, metals should be able to give up their electrons easily. Alkali metals, such as sodium and potassium, and alkaline earth metals, such as calcium and barium, do this the best. They almost never exist in pure form and will react with the oxygen in the air if purified.

▶ *Pieces of potassium. Potassium is so reactive with air that it has to be covered in unreactive mineral oil*

🔍 Transition Metals

These are what we commonly mean when we say metal. When they react with alkali metals, they can behave like non-metals. They are found in nature in a compound form called **ore** and can be converted to pure metal through a chemical process called refining. After refining, they stay in a pure state but react with the oxygen in the air very slowly by a process called corrosion. Some, such as gold and platinum, do not react at all and are known as noble metals.

💡 Isn't It Amazing!

For long, the toughest swords were said to come from the city of Damascus (present day capital of Syria), with beautiful patterns on the surface. They were made of wootz steel found in southern India. While the technique was lost for a period, some individuals have recreated techniques that are of the calibre of original Damascus steel.

▲ *An antique knife made of Damascus steel*

🔍 Alloys

An alloy is a mixture of metals that is stronger than either of them separately and is used for many purposes. Brass (copper and zinc), bronze (copper and tin), and stainless steel (iron and carbon) are the most common alloys.

Hydrogen and Helium

Did you know that 74% of the Universe is made of hydrogen (H), and another 8% is made of helium (He)? That just leaves 18% of the Universe's matter for the remaining 94 natural elements. But why is it so?

Hydrogen was the first element to be created when the Universe came into being during the Big Bang nearly 13.8 billion years ago. Therefore, it is called the mother of all elements. It is made of just one proton and one electron. It makes up the mass of all the stars, as well as a lot of **interstellar gas**. Deep inside stars, where the pressure is hundreds of millions of **pascals**, four hydrogens turn into one helium atom by a process called **nuclear fusion**. The electrons and protons of two atoms collapse into neutrons, which have no charge, while the other two protons join them to make the helium nucleus. The remaining two electrons form a pair that orbits around the new nucleus. A lot of energy is released from this reaction, making stars glow.

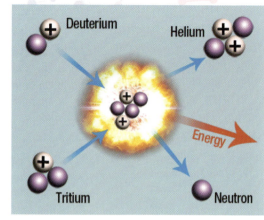

▲ Hydrogen turns into helium deep inside stars, giving the energy that makes them glow

Uses of Hydrogen

Elemental hydrogen is rarely found in nature as it is very reactive. It is produced industrially by making steam and methane (CH_4) react, with nickel (Ni) as a catalyst. This hydrogen is used for creating ammonia (NH_3), which is then used for making urea, which is used to make **fertilisers**. Hydrogen is also made to react with vegetable oils to turn them into margarine. These are just two of the numerous uses of hydrogen. It is also utilized in vehicles; in the production of electricity; in oil refineries; and so on.

◀ Margarine is made by making hydrogen react with vegetable oils

Isotopes of Hydrogen

Hydrogen has two isotopes. Deuterium is an isotope wherein the nucleus has a neutron in addition to a proton. As the electron has no weight, the deuterium nucleus is twice as heavy as the hydrogen nucleus. The isotope tritium has two neutrons, so it is thrice as heavy. Water that contains deuterium or tritium instead of plain hydrogen is called heavy water. It is used in nuclear reactors as a coolant.

Isn't It Amazing!

The Large Hadron Collider, a giant detector built by physicists to detect subatomic particles, uses 90 tons of liquid helium to maintain a temperature of -271.3°C.

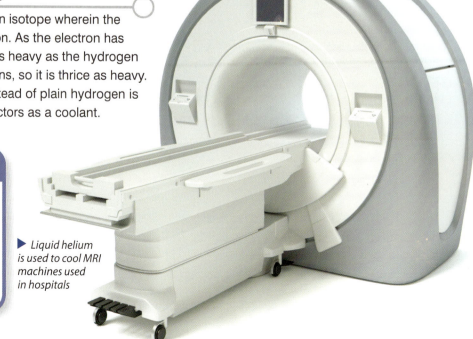

▶ Liquid helium is used to cool MRI machines used in hospitals

CHEMISTRY & ELEMENTS

Noble Gases

Look at the last column of the periodic table on pages 6–7. This clubs together the elements helium (He), neon (Ne), argon (Ar), krypton (Kr), xenon (Xe), radon (Rn), and oganesson (Og) as noble gases. But why are they called that?

Each row (called a **period**) of the periodic table represents one shell of an atom. A shell is the space in which electrons move. Every element that has its outermost shell completely filled with electrons will neither give up electrons nor take any. Thus, it becomes chemically unreactive. Since they do not form ionic, covalent, or hydrogen bonds, they have low boiling points and are gases at normal temperatures.

In earlier times, elements were classified as base, which reacted with others, and noble, which did not react with anything. Gold is a noble metal because it does not react with anything. Iron is a base metal because it reacts with oxygen from the air and **rusts**. That is how the noble gases got their name. All these are arranged at the end of the period and make a vertical group, since they have similar chemical properties.

86 **Radon** Rn

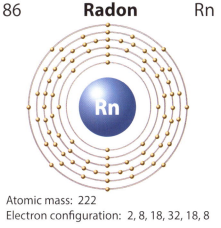

Row	Shells	Maximum Electrons in Outermost Shell	Elements
First	1	2	H, He
Second	2	8	Li to Ne
Third	3	8	Na to Ar
Fourth	4	18	K to Kr
Fifth	5	18	Rb to Xe
Sixth	6	32	Cs to Rn (including Lanthanides)
Seventh	7	32	Fr to Og (including Actinides)

Atomic mass: 222
Electron configuration: 2, 8, 18, 32, 18, 8

▲ An atom of radon showing all its 6 shells filled with electrons

💡 Isn't It Amazing!

Noble gases can be turned into plasma under very strong electric current. This plasma then glows with a signature colour. This property is used to make glowing lights, which are often used as shop signs. The first to be used was neon (Ne), which gives a reddish-orange colour. These lights are called neon lights. Other noble gases project different colours.

▲ Neon lights in Hong Kong. Different gases result in different colours when turned into plasma

Nitrogen

Making 78% of the air around you, nitrogen is the most abundant gas in the atmosphere, which is good for us for it is a chemically unreactive gas in molecular form (N_2). Without it acting as a **damp**, almost everything would burn easily in oxygen. On the other hand, as an element, nitrogen is extremely reactive. It makes both a powerful acid (nitric acid, HNO_3) and a powerful base (ammonia, NH_3). It is named after **nitre** (KNO_3), which is used in making explosives such as firecrackers.

Nitrogen is one of the six elements critical to life, being an important part of proteins and nucleic acids. However, if most of the nitrogen on our planet is inert, how does it become such an important part of our lives?

In Real Life

A number of bacteria can convert atmospheric nitrogen into ammonia, which is then used to make proteins and other biochemicals. Some of these bacteria live on their own, such as cyanobacteria. Others live together with plants such as legumes, inside a special structure in their roots, called root nodules. The plant gives them food in exchange for the ammonia that they make. Some of the ammonia is released into the soil. So farmers often grow a crop of legumes between other crops in order to enrich the soil with nitrogen again.

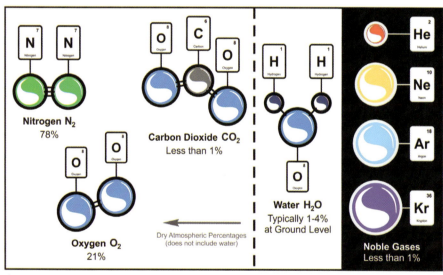

▲ The proportion of gases in our planet's atmosphere

▲ The root nodules of legumes contain bacteria that provide nitrogen for most living organisms through the food chain

Incredible Individuals

Carl Wilhelm Scheele (1742–1786) was a Swedish chemist who discovered many elements and compounds in his small laboratory. He discovered that air was made mostly of two gases—one that supported combustion (fire air), and another that did not (foul air), which we now know to be oxygen and nitrogen, respectively. Unfortunately, though he discovered chlorine, molybdenum, barium, tungsten, and hydrogen, he could never publish his discoveries in scientific journals, and the credit for his discoveries went to others. Today, however, he is recognised as one of the greatest chemists to have ever lived.

▶ Sweden printed a postal stamp in 1942 to recognise Scheele's 200th birthday

Oxygen

Though oxygen makes 21% of the atmosphere currently, did you know that there was no oxygen in the air three billion years ago? We owe the oxygen we breathe to certain blue-green bacteria that started making their own food through **photosynthesis** and released oxygen as a waste product. Although oxygen—like all other elements—is made in the stars by nuclear fusion, it is very reactive and becomes a part of various chemicals very quickly. Most of the oxygen on our planet is actually in the oceans, making 89% of seawater by weight.

▲ Blue-green bacteria, now part of pond scum or ocean plankton, made all the oxygen in the atmosphere today

Reactions of Life

Carbon is the main element that makes up all living organisms, but it is oxygen which takes part in the two great reactions that make up life. In photosynthesis, six molecules of water (H_2O) from the soil and six molecules of carbon dioxide (CO_2) from the air are combined in the presence of light to make one molecule of glucose ($C_6H_{12}O_6$). This reaction happens in blue-green bacteria, algae, and plants. Chlorophyll acts as the catalyst. Six molecules of oxygen (O_2) are released for each reaction and that's what we depend on for breathing.

$$6CO_2 + 6H_2O + light \rightarrow C_6H_{12}O_6 + 6O_2$$

The other great reaction is **respiration**, which happens in all living creatures. In photosynthetic creatures, it happens when there is no light. It is the exact reverse of photosynthesis, where glucose ($C_6H_{12}O_6$) reacts with oxygen (O_2) to form water (H_2O) and carbon dioxide (CO_2). Respiration turns the stored energy of light into the **chemical energy** that enables creatures to grow and move.

$$C_6H_{12}O_6 + 6O_2 \rightarrow 6CO_2 + 6H_2O + chemical\ energy$$

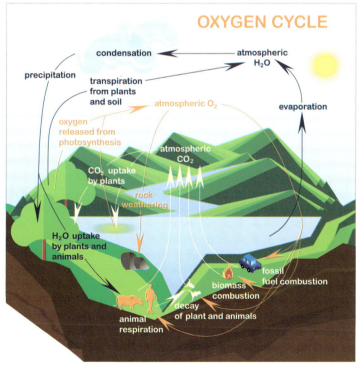

▲ The natural oxygen cycle between photosynthesis and respiration has now been disturbed by large-scale burning of fossil fuels

Incredible Individuals

Oxygen was discovered by Joseph Priestley (1733–1804) and confirmed by his friend Antoine Lavoisier (1743–94). Lavoisier gave oxygen its name after he discovered that it is a part of many acids. In Greek, *oxys* means acid and *genes* means parent, so oxygen stands for that which gives rise to acids. Both Priestley and Lavoisier led difficult lives. Lavoisier was beheaded in the French Revolution, and Priestley had to flee England due to his political views.

▲ We know much about oxygen due to the pioneering work of Joseph Priestley and Antoine Lavoisier

Carbon

Carbon (C) is the element that makes us. Together with oxygen (O) and hydrogen (H), it makes the carbohydrates and fats that we eat. Twenty kinds of special compounds made of C, H, O, and nitrogen, called amino acids, make all the proteins in our body. Deoxyribose Nucleic Acid (DNA) is a complicated compound made of phosphorus (P) and all these elements. DNA is the chemical that stores our genetic code. Other compounds of carbon form the vitamins we need and a whole lot of other biochemicals in our body. To understand why carbon is so special, we must look at its atomic structure.

Atomic Structure

The carbon nucleus is made of six protons and six neutrons. It has two shells of electrons, one pair of electrons in the inner shell, and four unpaired electrons in the outer. The four unpaired electrons are always looking for a partner, which determines its **valency**. So, a carbon atom can make chemical bonds with four other atoms, which makes it a tetravalent element. Very often, the carbon atom will link to another carbon atom through a covalent bond. In this way, carbon atoms can make a long chain called a concatenation. Sometimes, the chain folds in on itself, forming a ring of carbon atoms.

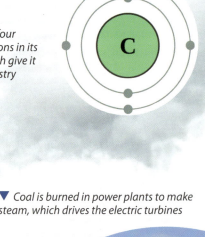

▶ Carbon has four unpaired electrons in its outer shell which give it a unique chemistry

Isn't It Amazing!

Diamonds are a complex compound made entirely of carbon atoms in which each atom is bound to four others. This makes the compound very compact and so diamond is the hardest thing on Earth. On the other hand, another form of carbon is graphite, in which carbon atoms form rings of six each and these rings make flat sheets. The sheets are stacked one upon another, so they can slip and slide. This makes graphite one of the softest materials known to man.

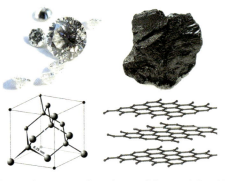

▲ The chemical structures of graphite and diamond. Graphite is used in pencils, while diamond is used for cutting metal sheets

▼ Coal is burned in power plants to make steam, which drives the electric turbines

Coal

Coal is made from the remains of plants that died millions of years ago and were reduced to elemental carbon over time. Coal is used for various purposes; one such use is as fuel in electric power plants. Coal and petroleum are together known as **fossil fuels**.

CHEMISTRY & ELEMENTS

formaldehyde   ethanol   quinine   benzene   cholesterol

acetylsalicylic acid   DDT   acetone   triclosan

▲ Carbon atoms are shown as points in large organic compounds to save space. Unsaturated bonds are shown as double or triple lines

🔍 Organic Compounds

There are several millions of compounds that can be made from carbon and thus it has its own field of chemistry called organic chemistry. Any chemical compound that has carbon and hydrogen atoms in it is an organic compound, though compounds containing only carbon and hydrogen are called hydrocarbons. Most hydrocarbons are obtained from petroleum, which is actually a mixture of hundreds of hydrocarbons found underground, or under the sea floor in many places around our planet.

Organic compounds containing other elements, such as oxygen, chlorine, or sulphur, can be made from hydrocarbons through chemical reactions. Hydrocarbons can be classified into two types:

1. Aliphatic compounds are made of carbon atoms lined up in long chains to which hydrogen atoms are attached. They are saturated and joined by a single bond. Chemicals such as acetone and ethanol are aliphatic compounds.

2. Aromatic compounds have their carbon atoms arranged in a ring. They are very stable and easily react with other substances. Chemicals such as benzene and quinine are aromatic compounds.

Organic compounds may be **saturated** or **unsaturated**. In saturated compounds, each carbon atom makes covalent bonds with four different atoms. In unsaturated compounds, there may be two or three covalent bonds between two carbon atoms. Most vegetable oils are unsaturated while the main compound in butter—butyric acid—is saturated.

Organic compounds are divided into two parts—a hydrocarbon backbone and functional groups. The backbone gives the compound its structure, while the functional groups such as acid (COOH), alcohol (-OH), amide ($CONH_2$) give it its chemical properties.

▲ Coal is a finite resource, as new coal takes over a million years to form. Most of the coal we use today is over 300 million years old

Sulphur and Phosphorus

Among non-metals, sulphur (S) and phosphorus (P) stand out for their usefulness, in both industry and biology. Sulphur is part of cysteine, an amino acid. which is part of keratin, the protein which makes your hair and nails. Sulphur atoms in cystine form disulphide bridges, which tie two strands of keratin together, making the hair stronger.

On the other hand, phosphorus is an important part of DNA, where it forms the 'backbone' of the molecule. It is also part of adenosine triphosphate (ATP), a compound that stores the energy released from respiration. Our bodies 'couple' reactions, so that every time there is a need for energy in a reaction (say adding an amino acid to a protein chain), ATP is broken down to adenosine diphosphate (ADP) and a free phosphate (PO_4^{3-}) ion:

Protein chain + amino acid + ATP → longer protein chain + ADP + PO_4^{3-}

▲ *The progress of a country is at times measured by the amount of sulphuric acid it uses*

🔍 Sulphuric Acid

Scientists call sulphuric acid (H_2SO_4) the 'king of chemicals' because it is part of several reactions that are important to modern life. It is found in most cars as part of the lead-acid battery that gives electric power to the engine. The electric power is used to create a spark, which makes the fuel burn inside the engine, making it work. Sulphuric acid is also used for manufacturing hundreds of chemicals, including phosphate fertilisers. It is also used in the manufacture of other acids, the refining of petroleum, and the solubilising of ores.

🔍 Phosphate Fertilisers

Ammonium phosphate (($NH_4)_3HPO_4$) is a common fertiliser that provides plants with both nitrogen (N) and phosphorus (P). It is made by treating two parts of ammonia (NH_3) with one part of phosphoric acid (H_3PO_4):

$$H_3PO_4 + 3NH_3 \rightarrow (NH_4)_3PO_4$$

▼ *Using phosphate fertilisers makes it possible to grow more crops in the same amount of land*

👤 In Real Life

Rubber is used widely to make tyres because it is elastic, strong, flexible, and light. However, natural rubber is prone to wearing off quickly unless it is vulcanised, which requires heating it with sulphur in large vats. The sulphur forms sulphide bridges between different rubber molecules, thus toughening it. This process was accidently discovered by Charles Goodyear in 1839.

Silicon, Semiconductors, and Ceramics

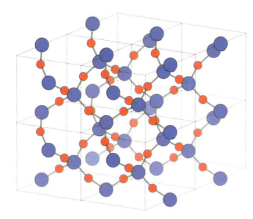

If you see the periodic table on pages 6–7, you will notice that silicon (Si) is placed in the same group (4A) as carbon. Elements in the same group (that is a vertical column of the periodic table) share similar chemical properties. Therefore, silicon, like carbon, is tetravalent, that is, it has four electrons to share. Like carbon, it also forms long chains. Silica (SiO_2), formed of silicon, and oxygen, is the most common compound in the crust of our planet, making up about 26% of it, and is found in sand, mud, and most rocks. Like diamond, it forms tetrahedral crystals called quartz.

◀ *The beautiful crystals of quartz are made from the tetrahedral arrangement of silicon dioxide molecules*

🔍 Semiconductors

If you look at the periodic table, you'll notice that silicon is part of a set of elements called metalloids, spread across periods and columns. All of them share a common property—they act as semiconductors of electricity. This means that they only allow a certain amount of current to pass through. Semiconductors are used today in a wide variety of electronics such as mobile phones, computers, and radiation sensors, among others.

▶ *An electronic board with a silicon chip in the centre will have millions of microscopic electronic circuits in it*

🔍 Ceramics

You see silicon all around your house—in the floor and wall tiles, in flowerpots and decorative vases, and even in the bricks that make your house. All of these are made of ceramics—things that are hardy, have low electric conductivity, and are chemically inert. They've been with us ever since the late Stone Age.

Clay from riverbeds is made of oxides of silicon and aluminium. These can be mixed with water to make a smooth dough that can be pressed into various shapes. When the moulded objects are dried and heated at a high temperature in a **kiln**, the silicon oxides form various interlinking structures that give the material its hardness but also make it brittle, that is, easily breakable.

▲ *A potter's wheel is used to shape wet clay before it is baked*

👤 In Real Life

Supercooling happens when a liquid is cooled below freezing point but hasn't turned solid. Glass is supercooled silica, but it is so viscous that it behaves like an amorphous solid.

▶ *The art of stained-glass painting involves painting on glass pieces and heating them in a kiln so that the paint becomes transparent*

Currency Metals

Look at column 1B in the periodic table. It has the three metals: copper (Cu, from Latin *cuprum*), silver (Ag, from Latin *argentum*), and gold (Au, from Latin *aurum*). They are called currency metals, because they were used for making coins for a long time. They share similar properties of being very ductile (can be drawn into wires) and malleable (can be hammered into shapes).

Gold is often alloyed with silver or copper to make it more malleable, because pure gold can break on hammering. They also make it less dense and therefore, lighter. The purity of gold is measured in carats, with 24 carats being the purest form possible (99.9%). Most jewellery is 18 carats (75%), with 25% silver or copper.

▲ Lumps of gold, copper, and silver. Due to certain scarcities, coupled with growing demand, the price for copper has shot up recently

🔍 Corrosion

Corrosion is an occurrence wherein metals react with the air while water vapour acts as a catalyst. When silver corrodes, it is called **tarnish**. It reacts with hydrogen sulphide (H_2S) present in air to form silver sulphide (Ag_2S), which is black in colour. Copper reacts with the carbon dioxide present in damp air to form a greenish **patina**. When iron corrodes, it is called **rust**. But as long as metal objects are kept dry, they stay as they are. Gold does not react with anything except when it is pressurised under extreme conditions. That is why it was used as money since it does not lose its value.

▲ Did you know that the Statue of Liberty is green because it is made of copper which has acquired a patina?

👤 In Real Life

Numismatics is the art and science of studying coins. It can tell us a lot about life in the past, including the prices of things and how countries were governed.

▲ Collecting coins is a very interesting hobby

🔍 Other Metals and Alloys

Since 1866, the 5-cent coins of the USA have been made of nickel (Ni), and hence are called nickels. In our times, alloys of copper and nickel (cupro-nickel), stainless steel, zinc, and aluminium are used to make coins. Bronze (an alloy of copper and tin) and brass (an alloy of copper and zinc) are also used.

▲ These coins are part of the European currency. Modern coins are made from a wide variety of metals and alloys

Iron and Steel

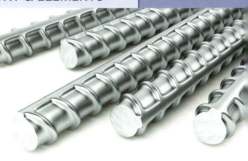

The uses of iron and steel are so many that they would need a book of their own. Iron is a wonder metal. It is hard yet not brittle; it is ductile and malleable; and it is a great conductor of heat and electricity.

The science of metallurgy looks at how metals are purified (extracted) from their natural state. In nature, a metal is part of a compound, usually an oxide, sulphate, nitrate, or phosphate. These compounds are called minerals. Rocks are made of minerals of various kinds. The rocks that are rich in the mineral of a particular metal are called ores. The most common ores of iron are hematite (Fe_2O_3) and magnetite (Fe_3O_4).

Extraction of metal from an ore is called smelting. The ore is crushed to powder and mixed with flux, a chemical that reacts with the ore and reduces it to metal. For iron, a pure form of coal called coke is used. The ore and flux are melted in a smelter and the following reaction takes place:

$$Fe_3O_4 + 2C \rightarrow 3Fe + 2CO_2 \text{ and } Fe_2O_3 + 3CO \rightarrow 2Fe + 3CO_2$$

The pure iron is usually allowed to solidify as **ingots**.

Isn't It Amazing!

In Delhi, the capital city of India, there is a pillar made of iron that has not rusted ever since it was built more than 1,600 years ago. This is because it is covered by a thin film of iron hydrogen phosphate ($FeHPO_4$) which stops air from reacting with the iron underneath.

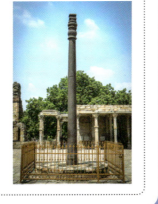

▶ The Iron Pillar in Delhi

▶ Molten refined iron being poured into rods which will be cut into rectangular ingots

Steel

Most of the iron in the world is used as steel, an alloy that has up to 2% carbon and manganese. Carbon makes steel harder and less brittle than iron. Steel does not rust as easily as iron, and is more malleable and ductile. That is why it is used to make train tracks, bridges, vehicles of all kinds, and even cooking vessels. When steel rods are used as a frame over which cement is poured, it is called reinforced cement concrete (RCC).

Alloy Name	Carbon %	Manganese %	Used to make
Very Low Carbon Steel	0.1	0.4	Car body panels
Low Carbon Steel	0.1 – 0.3	1.5	Stamped and forged things
Medium Carbon Steel	0.3 – 0.6	0.6 – 1.65	Railway wheels and rails
High Carbon Steel	0.6 – 1.0	0.3 – 0.9	Springs and high-strength wires

Polymers, Plastics, and Rubber

So far we have seen how carbon atoms can link to themselves, forming long chains. They can also form long chains (polymers) of whole molecules called **monomers**. A **polymer** may be made of the same kind of molecule or one kind of monomeric unit called a homopolymer. For example, starch is made of glucose molecules linked together. If a polymer is made of different kinds of molecules, such as amino acids in a protein, it is called a heteropolymer. While nature makes many complex polymers, humans too have found ways to make them. Many of them have special industrial uses but some of them have become common in our lives—plastics, rubber, and synthetic fabrics.

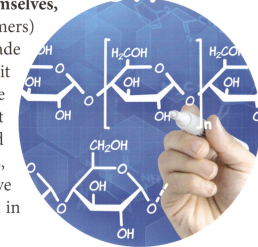

▲ Starch is a homopolymer made of glucose molecules that are its monomers

Petrochemicals

Petroleum is formed from the carbohydrates of dead plants and animals that were buried millions of years ago. In modern times, it is pumped out from the ground in **oil wells** (on land) or **oil rigs** (at sea). When it goes through fractional distillation (see page 11), it gives many different chemicals. Some of these are used as fuel in our cars, airplanes, and rockets, such as petrol (called gasoline in the USA), diesel, kerosene, and naphtha. A whole lot of others are used as raw materials to make petrochemicals. These include plastics of all kinds, paints, dyes, synthetic fabrics like nylon, vinyl, and synthetic rubber.

Plastics are made from monomers obtained from petroleum. The polymers may be in the form of long chains or branched networks of monomers. Long-chain polymers are favoured for making synthetic fabrics such as nylon. Branched polymers are preferred for making moulded items. Bakelite, a highly branched polymer (which makes it tough), is used for making brake pads, toys, and electric insulation.

Plastics are often named after the monomer used to make them. For example, PET, used to make bottles and food boxes, is Poly-Ethylene Terephthalate, and PVC, used for making pipes, is Poly Vinyl Chloride. Polyethylene is used for making disposable plastic bags and Polystyrene is used for disposable cups. They are now banned in many countries.

▼ An oil rig pumps out petroleum from the sea floor and a giant ship called a tanker carries it to the shore where the petroleum is refined into fuels and petrochemicals

CHEMISTRY & ELEMENTS

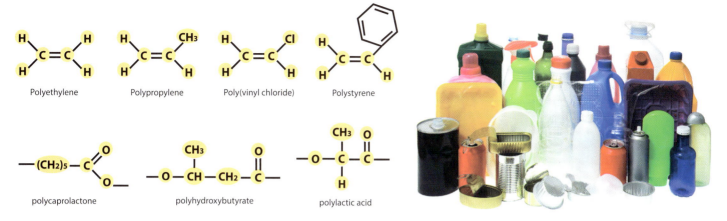

▲ Petrochemicals (left) are used as monomers to make a wide variety of plastics (right) and synthetic fabrics

Rubber

Rubber is a natural polymer made from the rubber tree. It has many uses in our lives, though most of it is used to make vehicle tyres. Rubber is also used to make gloves and waterproof clothing, insulation for electrical items, carpets, and also the erasers used to remove pencil marks. Indeed, that is how rubber gets its name in English.

The monomer of rubber is a compound called cis-polyisoprene. It is made from the rubber tree, *Hevea brasiliensis*. Synthetic rubber is made from a similarly shaped compound called butadiene.

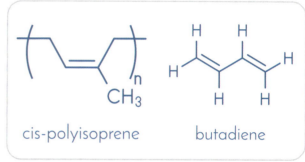

▲ The monomers of natural rubber (left) and synthetic rubber (right)

Incredible Individuals

Thousands of police officers and soldiers owe their lives to one woman—scientist Stephanie Kwolek (1923–2014). She invented a polymer called Poly-p-phenylene terephthalamide, which she found was resistant to tearing and breaking even by bullets. This polymer can be turned into a fabric called Kevlar, which is sewn into bulletproof vests.

▲ Bulletproof vests are made of a polymer called Kevlar, invented by Stephanie Kwolek

▲ Natural rubber is made from the sap of rubber trees

Nuclear Chemistry

On page 18, you read about nuclear fusion that happens deep within stars. There is another kind of **nuclear reaction** called **radioactive decay**, seen in the elements technetium (Tc), promethium (Pm), and all elements beyond bismuth. The atoms break down spontaneously into a smaller atom and an alpha particle, which is made of two protons and two neutrons (like a helium nucleus). For example, uranium (U, atomic weight 238, atomic number 92) decays into thorium (Th), releasing energy.

$$^{238}U_{92} \rightarrow {}^{234}Th_{90} + {}^{4}He_{2} + \text{energy}$$

There is another kind of radioactive decay, in which a neutron suddenly breaks up into a proton and a **beta particle** (similar to an electron). The atomic weight stays the same, but the atomic number goes up. For example, thorium beta decays into protactinium (Pa).

$$^{234}Th_{90} \rightarrow {}^{234}Pa_{91} + e^{-} + \text{energy}$$

🔍 Chain Reaction

The physicist Enrico Fermi discovered that if a neutron was shot at a nucleus, like a bullet at a target, it could make the nucleus break into two and release energy along with a few more neutrons. This is called nuclear fission. The released neutrons then hit other nuclei and break them up and so the process goes on and on. This is called a chain reaction. Nuclear fission chain reactions can be made to happen in a special building called a nuclear reactor. The energy thus released is then used to boil water to make steam, which turns a turbine, generating electricity. This is how a nuclear power plant works.

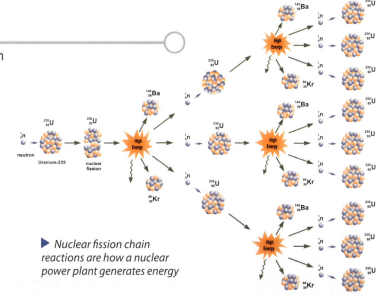

▶ *Nuclear fission chain reactions are how a nuclear power plant generates energy*

💡 Isn't It Amazing!

Did you know that out there in the Universe, there are stars that are made entirely of neutrons? They act like giant magnets and give out X-rays rather than light!

▲ *Rotating neutron stars are also called pulsars*

🏅 Incredible Individuals

Marie Sklodowska Curie (1867–1934) was a physicist and chemist who conducted pioneering research on radioactivity. She was the first woman to become a professor at the University of Paris. She discovered radioactive decay, as well as the elements polonium (Po; which she named after her birth country Poland) and radium (Ra). She received the Nobel Prize for Physics in 1903, and the Nobel Prize for Chemistry in 1911.

▶ *Marie Curie discovered radioactivity*

Green Chemistry

In the last two centuries, humankind has made a lot of progress. Developments in the field of Chemistry led to much of the progress, providing several new forms of materials and discovering new reactions. However, not all ideas have turned out so well. While plastics have been of great use in our daily lives, today they are polluting our forests and oceans, killing many innocent creatures. The CO_2 emitted by fossil fuels is causing global warming while many other chemicals that escape into the atmosphere cause acid rain and severe allergies. Today, chemists around the world are trying to find ways to reduce and even reverse these pollution-related problems.

▲ Plastics kill thousands of sea creatures each year

Fuel Cells

A fuel cell works much like an electric cell. But unlike an electric cell, a fuel cell uses hydrogen and oxygen gases instead of a solid anode and cathode. Inside the cell, the gases react with each other to form water and release chemical energy in the process. This energy is converted into electrical energy. In a fuel cell vehicle (FCV), the electricity is used to move the wheels. As these cars emit only water vapour, they cause no pollution.

Nevertheless, scientists are yet to find ways to generate fuel cells on a large scale.

▲ Fuel cells make hydrogen gas react with oxygen to make electric power, releasing water instead of smoke

Biodegradables

Most natural chemicals decay. Metals corrode, termites eat wood, leather and cloth disintegrate in soil. However, nothing like this happens to plastics and they remain on our planet for millions of years. Many scientists have worked to replace regular plastic material with something which will disintegrate easily on its own in the presence of light or by the action of bacteria. Other scientists are experimenting with materials made from natural sources such as starch, cellulose, and wheat gluten. These are hardy and can withstand the pressures of daily life, but once discarded, these will degrade into simple chemicals such as carbon dioxide and water.

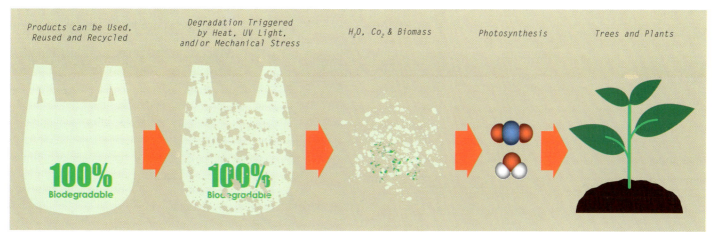

▲ A biodegradable product can be broken down by bacteria and fungi into recyclable natural compounds

Word Check

Antacid: A chemical that counters the action of acid in the stomach

Beta Particle: A weightless, negatively charged subatomic particle

Centrifuge: A machine used to separate undissolved solids from a liquid by spinning

Chemical Energy: The energy stored in the form of a chemical bond between the atoms of a molecule

Chemical Reaction: An exchange of electrons between two elements or compounds

Damp: A material that reduces the rate of chemical reactions, especially burning

Fertiliser: A chemical that is added to soil to provide additional nutrients to plants

Fossil Fuel: Fuel made from the remains of plants and animals that died millions of years ago

Hydroxyl Ion: An ion made of an oxygen atom and a hydrogen atom, with a net negative charge, that is made by alkalis

Ingot: A block of pure metal

Interstellar Gas: Gas that exists in space and is not part of stars or the atmosphere of planets

Kiln: A special kind of oven in which ceramics are hardened

Monomer: An organic compound that can react with its own molecules to form a polymer

Nitre: A common name for potassium nitrate, used in making explosives.

Nuclear Fusion: A nuclear reaction in which the nuclei of atoms merge to form new elements

Nuclear Reaction: A reaction by which the nuclei of atoms give out energy by splitting apart

Oil Rig: A facility for pumping out petroleum from the seabed

Oil Well: A facility for pumping out petroleum from the ground

Orbital: The space in which an electron revolves around the nucleus of its atom

Ore: A mineral from which metal can be extracted on a large scale

Pascal: The unit for measuring pressure, defined as one Newton of force applied over an area of one square metre

Patina: Corrosion of a metal that leaves a coloured compound on its surface

Period: A row of the periodic table in which all elements have a common outer shell

Photosynthesis: The creation of glucose in living organisms from water and carbon dioxide, which stores energy from sunlight

Polymer: A chemical made of repeating units of a simpler compound called a monomer

Proteins: Compounds made by linking together different kinds of amino acids in a long chain

Radioactivity or Radioactive Decay: The process by which a giant nucleus gives out an alpha or beta particle

Reactivity: The ease with which an element or compound reacts with other chemicals

Respiration: The breakdown of glucose in living organisms to water and carbon dioxide, which releases energy

Rust: Corrosion of iron in damp air that leaves brown iron oxide on its surface

Salt: A compound formed by the reaction of an acid with a base

Saturated: An organic compound in which each carbon atom is bound to four different atoms

Solvent: A substance that dissolves another substance

Supersaturation: A solution which has crossed the maximum amount a substance will dissolve in it

Tarnish: Corrosion of silver that leaves black silver sulphide on its surface

Unsaturated: An organic compound in which at least two carbon atoms are bound to each other by two or three covalent bonds

Valency: The number of electrons an atom can spare for chemical reactions

Viscosity: The resistance a substance offers to flowing

Image Credits

a: above, b: below/bottom, c: centre, f: far, l: left, r: right, t: top, bg: background

Cover
Shutterstock: Sergey Nivens; isak55; Chatchawal Kittirojana; Romolo Tavani; Shebeko; Theeraphong; zhu difeng; Alexx60; Shestakov Dmytro; Bjoern Wylezich

Wikimedia Commons:

Inside
Shutterstock: 3b/Romolo Tavani; 4&5c/Vector FX; 4b/Szasz-Fabian Ilka Erika; 5tr/everything possible; 5bg/pro500; 5br/amirage; 6&7 c/ollomy; 7bl/Nasky; 8tr/Fouad A. Saad; 8b/tony mills; 9tr/Marc Rossmann; 9cl/PHIL LENOIR; 9br/Standret; 10tl/Okrasiuk; 10cr/Serenethos; 10b/Dmitri Ma; 11tr/Steve Cymro; 11cr/Yuttasak Chuntarothai; 11bc/Paul Hakimata Photography; 13tr/VectorMine; 14bl/Serj Malomuzh; 14&15c/Designua; 15tr/Theeraphong; 15br1/Alhovik; 15br/MilanB; 16cl/Crevis; 16br/VectorMine; 17tr/ppart; 17br/ilozavr; 18cl/mipan; 18br/abramsdesign; 19cr/White Space Illustrations; 19br/Michal Ludwiczak; 20cl/udaix; 20bg/Alena Ohneva; 20cr/Kazakova Maryia; 21tr/fujilovers; 21bl/danylyukk1; 22bc/YURY STROK; 22br/Chatchawal Kittirojana; 23tl1/StudioMolekuul; 23tl2/StudioMolekuul; 23tl3/StudioMolekuul; 23tl4/StudioMolekuul; 23tc1/StudioMolekuul; 23tc2/StudioMolekuul; 23tc3/StudioMolekuul; 23tr1/StudioMolekuul; 23br2/StudioMolekuul; 23b/xpixel; 24cl/Lakeview Images; 24b/SAM THOMAS A; 25tl/StudioMolekuul; 25cr/raigvi; 25br/svekloid; 26tr/Bjoern Wylezich; 26cl/spyarm; 26cr/Erkipauk; 26b/Andrey Lobachev; 27tr/Oleksandr_Delyk; 27cl/Kaarthikeyan.SM; 27cr/Shestakov Dmytro; 28tr/Zerbor; 28b/Mohammad Fahmi Abu Bakar; 29tl/Mari-Leaf; 29tr/Josep Curto; 29cr1/StudioMolekuul; 29cr1/StudioMolekuul; 29bl/FeyginFoto; 29br/Manusphoto; 30cr/MPanchenko; 30bl/Jurik Peter; 31tr/Rich Carey; 31cr/metamorworks; 31b/Orakunya

Wikimedia Commons: 5cr/File:Helium-Bohr.svg//wikimedia commons; 6br/File:Biographies of Scientific Men 167 Mendeleev.jpg/File:Biographies of Scientific Men.djvu, Public domain, via Wikimedia Commons/wikimedia commons; 12cl/udaix; 13br/File:Dalton John desk.jpg/Henry Roscoe (author), William Henry Worthington (engraver), and Joseph Allen (painter), Public domain, via Wikimedia Commons/wikimedia commons; 17cr///wikimedia commons; 18tl/File:Nuclear fusion.gif/Someone, CC BY-SA 3.0 <https://creativecommons.org/licenses/by-sa/3.0/>, via Wikimedia Commons/wikimedia commons; 19bc/File:SeoulLights.jpg/Chitrapa at English Wikipedia, Public domain, via Wikimedia Commons/wikimedia commons; 20br/File:Carl Wilhelm Scheele.png/Ida Falander (1842—1927), Public domain, via Wikimedia Commons/wikimedia commons; 21bc/File:Priestley.jpg/English: Ellen Sharples (1769 - 1849)한국어: 엘렌 샤플즈 (1769 - 1849), Public domain, via Wikimedia Commons/wikimedia commons; 21br/File:Lavoisier 1877.png/Unknown authorUnknown author, Public domain, via Wikimedia Commons/wikimedia commons; 22cl/File:Diamond and graphite2.jpg/Diamond_and_graphite.jpg: User:Itubderivative work: Materialscientist, CC BY-SA 3.0 <http://creativecommons.org/licenses/by-sa/3.0/>, via Wikimedia Commons/wikimedia commons; 22tr/File:Electron shell 006 Carbon.svg/Pumbaa (original work Greg Robson), CC BY-SA 2.0 UK <https://creativecommons.org/licenses/by-sa/2.0/uk/deed.en>, via Wikimedia Commons/wikimedia commons; 25bl/File:Pottenbakkersschijf.JPG/Oriel, Public domain, via Wikimedia Commons/wikimedia commons; 30br/Unknown authorUnknown author, Public domain, via Wikimedia Commons/Unknown authorUnknown author, Public domain, via Wikimedia Commons/wikimedia commons

Slipcase
Shutterstock: Andrey Armyagov; isak55; MedstockPhotos; Romolo Tavani; Pushish Images; Blue Planet Studio; Sergey Nivens; Kenneth Keifer; Billion Photos

KNOWLEDGE ENCYCLOPEDIA
CHEMISTRY & ELEMENTS

What makes up matter? What are the different state of matter? How do chemical reactions take place? This encyclopedia will answer these and more *whats* and *hows* for you. Learning is made simpler with well-labelled diagrams, and an extensive glossary of difficult words. Bonus: the book comes loaded with *Isn't It Amazing*—a section of fun facts to keep you glued for more.

Other titles in this series

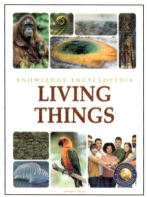
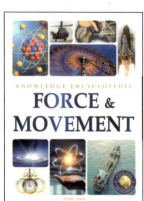

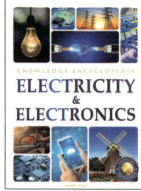
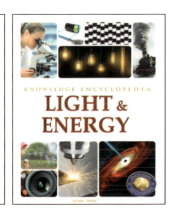

| UK £ 4.99 | CAN $ 7.99 | US $ 5.99 |

ISBN: 978-93-54401-60-2

Copyright © 2024 Wonder House Books
Wonder House Books is an imprint of
Prakash Books

www.wonderhousebooks.com

MRP
00019900

@wonderhousebooks   f wonderhousebooks   X wonderhousebook

EL ESTUDIO BÍBLICO PARA *Niños*

UNA DIVERTIDA MANERA DE APRENDER LA BIBLIA